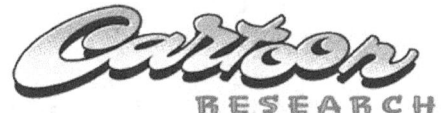

RESEARCH

PRESENTS

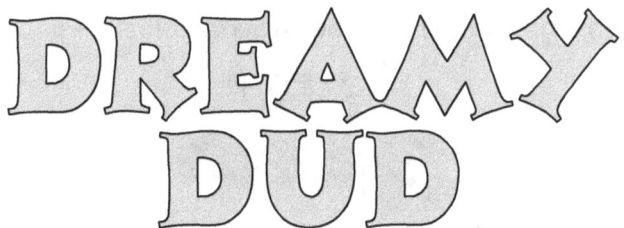

WALLACE A. CARLSON'S
ANIMATION CLASSIC

Compiled by Kevin Scott Collier

DREAMY DUD

WALLACE A. CARLSON'S ANIMATION CLASSIC

Compiled by Kevin Scott Collier

PRESENTED BY

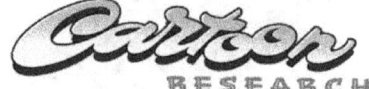

1020 North Hollywood Way #102
Burbank, California 91504
Visit us online:
www.cartoonresearch.com
Founder: Jerry Beck
Email: jerrybeck18@gmail.com

CARTOON FOREWORD

A Pioneering Cartoonist and Animator
Written by Kevin Scott Collier

My interest in Wallace Anderson Carlson arose from research regarding pioneering animator Winsor McCay. You see, McCay lived the first 18 years of his life not more than three miles from my residence in the village of Spring Lake, Michigan. He's our hometown hero.

I've lectured on McCay for 37 years, and am a member of the Spring Lake District Library's McCay committee. I also participate in the annual McCay Day events held there each June and teach area cartooning classes. My book, *Winsor McCay: Boyhood Dreams*, published in March 2017, documents the young illustrator's life here.

Wallace A. Carlson was a successful early animator whose work in the genre of film cartoons has gained interest over the past several decades, with DVD releases and online video hosting sites playing a role in his resurrection.

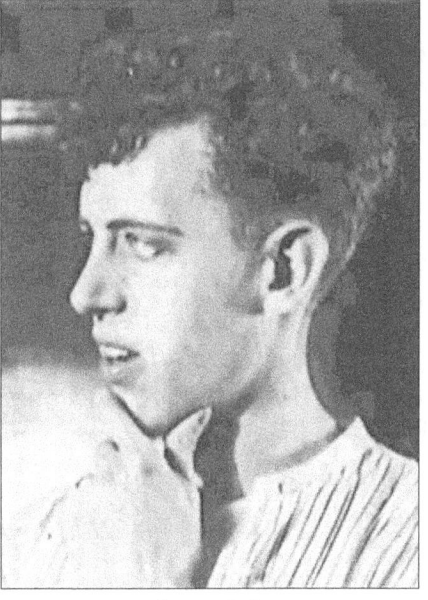

Wallace A. Carlson.
Bray Animation Project/Stathes Collection.

I want to thank Tommy José Stathes and Bray Animation Project/Stathes Collection for contribution and participation in this book.

Special thanks to Jerry Beck of Cartoon Research for his association with the distribution and promotion of this book.

Hopefully, this little book will further fuel interest in Carlson's legacy, not solely regarding the Dreamy Dud character, but for his entire body of animation work.

"While a series like Dreamy Dud will please the public for a while, I believe the future of the animated cartoon is in the showing of current events by drawings which will instruct as well as amuse. The movies are too great and durable to admit limitations. Why should not the screen become the world's most potent cartoon medium?"

- *Wallace A. Carlson*

CARLSON BIOGRAPHY

Wallace Anderson Carlson
1894-1967

Wallace Anderson Carlson, born on March 28, 1894, in St. Louis, Missouri, was the son of Peter and Annie (Ramlose), Carlson. His parents were both born in 1860, his father in Sweden, his mother in Denmark.

Peter Carlson had immigrated to the United States in 1883. His wife immigrated to the United States in 1877.

Peter Anderson was a tailor by trade. Wallace had three siblings, two older brothers, Victor and Carl, and a sister, Maude, who was three years younger than he.

The Carlson family resided at 4641 Bell Avenue in St. Louis, then moved to Chicago, Illinois in 1905, taking residence at 712 Aldine Avenue. The Carlson children attended public schools.

At the age of 12, Wallace Carlson was a newspaper delivery boy. His interest in art already attracted both attention and money. Carlson sold original baseball cartoons to a cigar store owner for 50 cents each, who put them on display in his shop window.

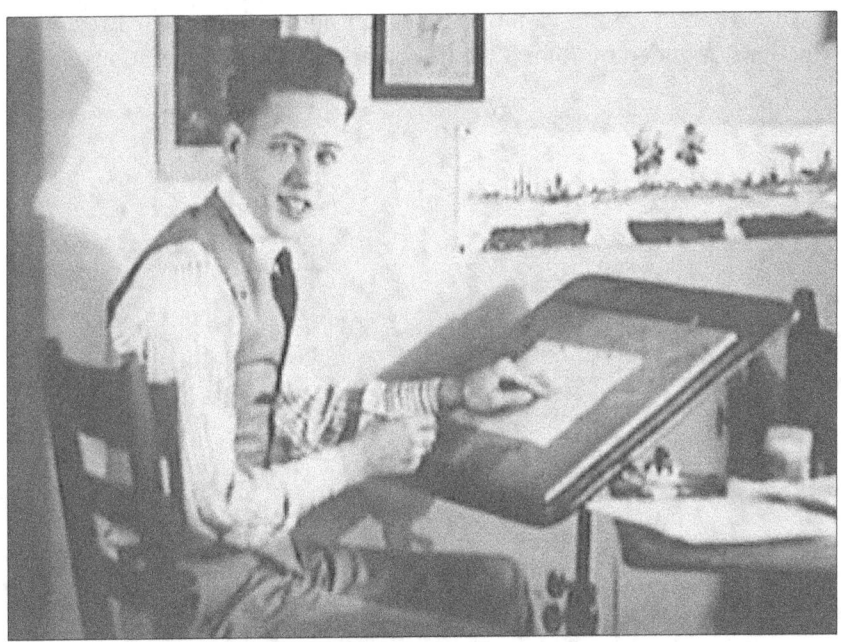

Wallace A. Carlson, 1919, Bray Animation Project/Stathes Collection.

At the age of 14, Carlson was a student at Lane Technical High School and sold cartoons to Chicago's Inter-Ocean newspaper. He graduated to a staff position in the paper's sports department, doing a daily sports comic and occasionally a front page political cartoon.

In a 1910 census his occupation, at the age of 16, was "cartoonist."

Carlson's father passed away in 1913, basically leaving him to help provide for his mother.

At an early age, Carlson discovered that drawing little skeletons at slightly different positions on the corners of pages in books, and then flipping the pages, made the figures move.

At the age of 17, Carlson took a job as an illustrator for The Chicago Herald for a short time, then entered the new world of film animation.

Carlson created his first animated cartoon work for the Historical Film Corporation. It was an animated depiction of the 1914 baseball World Series, which concluded on October 13 with the Boston Braves winning over the Philadelphia Athletics. The film was a lucrative venture that was sold outright to theaters for $50—an equivalent of $1,225 today.

His first film cartoon series as an illustrator and animator was "Joe Boko," in 1914 for Essanay Studios. His second for the company was "Dreamy Dud," which made its debut the following year.

In 1916, Carlson took a job as illustrator and animator for Bray Productions, founded by John R. Bray. Its central office of operation was at

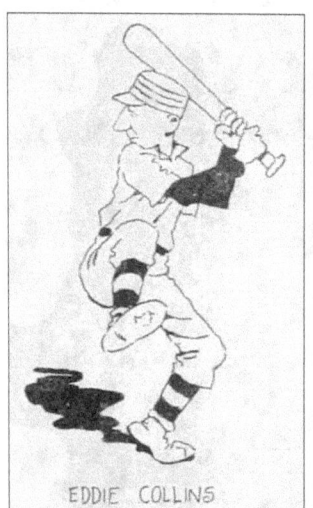 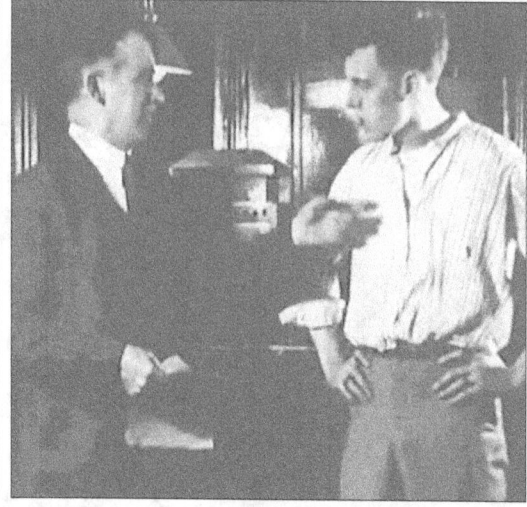

Left: 1914 World Series illustration for Historical Film Corporation. Right: John R. Bray exchanging ideas with Wallace A. Carlson, 1919, Bray Animation Project/Stathes Collection.

23 East 26th Street, New York, New York. Carlson maintained a residence at 424 Oakdale, Avenue, Chicago, Illinois.

Wallace Carlson continued "Dreamy Dud" for Bray Studios and while there created three cartoon series: "Goodrich Dirt" (1916), "Otto Luck" (1917), and "Us Fellers" (1919).

On his draft card dated May 13, 1917, Carlson indicates he was serving as a provider for his widowed mother and younger sibling.

"[I am supporting my] mother and sister largely, but not solely," Carlson wrote. "[My] family is practically dependent on me."

In 1918, Carlson appeared in Bray's short film "How Animated Car-

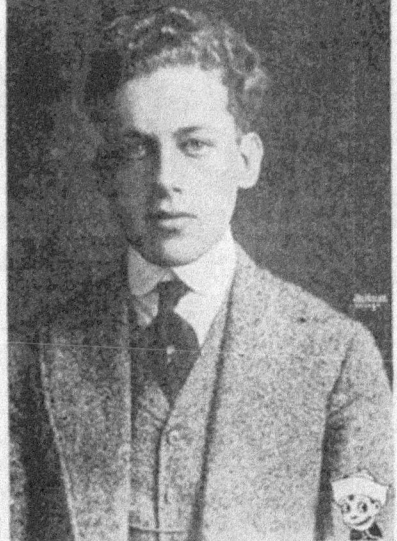

Wallace Carlson Joins Bray

WALLACE CARLSON, one of the first to enter the animated cartoon field, but still one of the youngest cartoonists in the business, has joined the staff of the Bray Studios, Inc., and his work in the future will be released by them as part of their production, the Paramount-Bray Pictograph, the "magazine-on-the-screen." Mr. Carlson has originated a new character, which he calls "Otto Luck," and unquestionably it will take rank in popular favor with J. R. Bray's famous Col. Heeza Liar and Earl Hurd's "Bobby Bumps," the cutest kid on the screen.

Mr. Carlson at fifteen years of age was the sporting cartoonist on the Chicago Inter-Ocean—one of America's foremost dailies—and held that position up to the time of his entrance in the animated cartoon field He is the originator of the "Canimated Nooz"—a burlesque on the news weeklies—and attained a wide popularity through this clever idea. His best known "movie" character was "Dreamy Dud"—a kid with an imagination that outdid anything that the late lamented Baron Munchausen ever approached.

Wallace Carlson.

The cleverness of Mr. Carlson's work, together with his extreme youth, attracted the attention of many prominent persons, and among his treasured possessions are letters from President Wilson and Judge Landis of Chicago, both commending his work.

The Moving Picture World magazine article, June 2, 1917.

toons Are Made," which depicts Carlson drawing and also his character Dreamy Dud. Company founder John R. Bray makes a cameo appearance.

Carlson once thought about being an actor, but was displeased upon seeing himself on the screen, so abandoned the notion.

Carlson was married twice in his life. He first married Rosalie Maeder in Chicago in March 1919. Wallace and Rosalie Carlson had one son, Richard. They resided at 4188 Clarendon Avenue.

In 1919 Carlson went into business for himself, establishing Carlson Studios. Wallace's brother Carl, who also worked as a commercial illustrator, was his co-partner in the venture.

Among its films, the company produced animated versions of Sidney Smith's "The Gumps" from 1920-21. Metro-Goldwyn-Mayer distributed the cartoons.

Afterward, Carlson departed the world of animation partnering with "The Gumps" writer Sol Hess to produce "The Nebbs." The Bell Syndicate distributed the comic strip to newspapers beginning May 1, 1923. Carlson also illustrated the Sunday companion piece, "Simp O'Dill."

Carlson's mother Annie passed away in 1928.

Wallace and his wife Rosalie divorced shortly after 1930. In Novem-

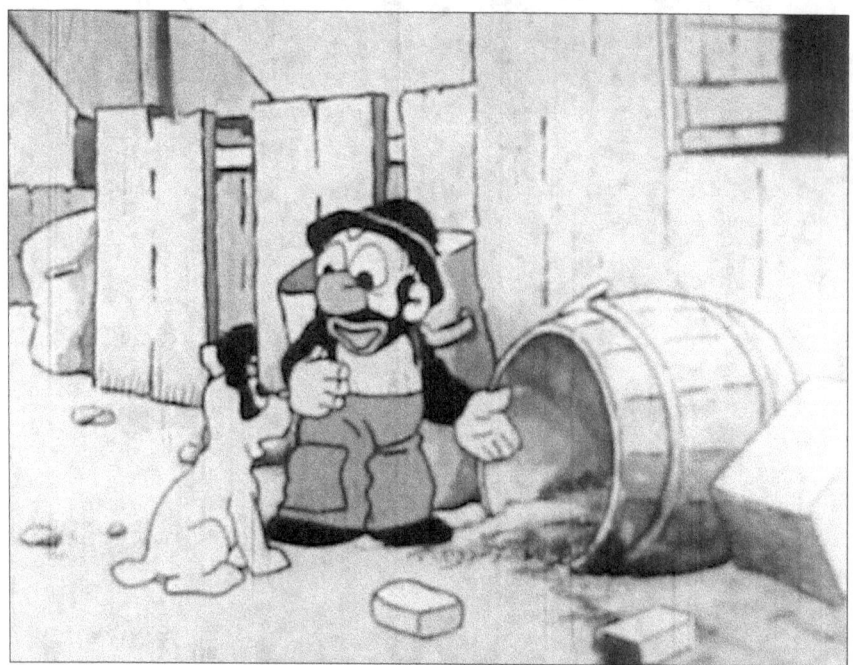

"Goodrich Dirt" cartoon frame, 1919, Bray Animation Project/Stathes Collection.

8

ber 1933 Carlson remarried. His second wife, Patricia (Edenton) Carlson, had three children from a previous marriage: LaVerne, Stephanie, and Jack.

The Carlsons lived at 2613 Hampden Court, Chicago, then nearby 3020 Sheridan Road.

By World War II, Carlson had carved out a successful career illustrating "The Nebbs" as a comic strip artist and was working for Rae Hess, the widow of Sol Hess, who passed away in 1941.

"The Nebbs" was subsequently written by Hess' daughter and son-in-law. Carlson ceased as the comic strip's artist in 1946.

That same year Carlson created and illustrated the single-panel daily comic, and Sunday strip, "Mostly Malarky." Art Huhta assisted him, and also helped on later "The Nebbs" comic strips.

Carlson was a gifted amateur magician noted for his versatility and funny dialect stories. He also enjoyed a secret concerning the two cleaning ladies portrayed in "Mostly Malarky." He would never reveal which one was named Mazie and would only say, "the other one was Daisy."

In his twilight years, Carlson resided at 739 Brompton Place, Chicago.

Wallace A. Carlson died as a result of a heart attack on May 9, 1967, in Chicago, Illinois. He had been dining at a restaurant on May 5 when suffering chest pains and rushed to St. Joseph's Hospital, where he remained in a coma until his passing.

The final edition of "Mostly Malarky" was published a couple of months later on July 30 that year.

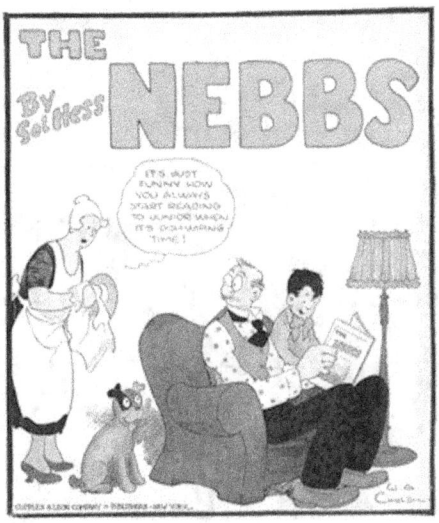 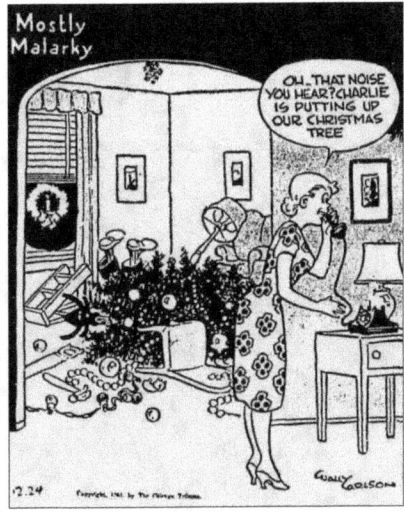

Left: Carlson illustration for "The Nebbs." Right: Carlson's "Mostly Malarky" comic strip.

CARLSON'S SIGNIFICANCE

Tommy José Stathes
Bray Animation Project/Stathes Collection

Tommy José Stathes is an internationally recognized archivist, historian, distributor, and educator in the realm of early animated and silent films. As the man behind the Bray Animation Project/Stathes Collection, Stathes is well versed on the work and influence of Dreamy Dud and its creator, Wallace A. Carlson.

"Wallace Carlson's role as a pioneer in early animation is noteworthy, although it has likely been an obscure anecdote ever since he exited the world of animation—at a time when animation as an industry was still in its overall infancy," Stathes explained. "Carlson's 'Canimated Nooz Pictorial' and 'Dreamy Dud' series for the Essanay Studios is significant for the simple reason that it gave Chicago a stake in early animation history, whereas most of the milestones occurred in New York and California."

Stathes noted Carlson's "Us Fellers" in particular, which presented a continuation of Dreamy Dud's adventures after the creator retired the series title, as developing a legacy for the animator that helped birth the animation industry.

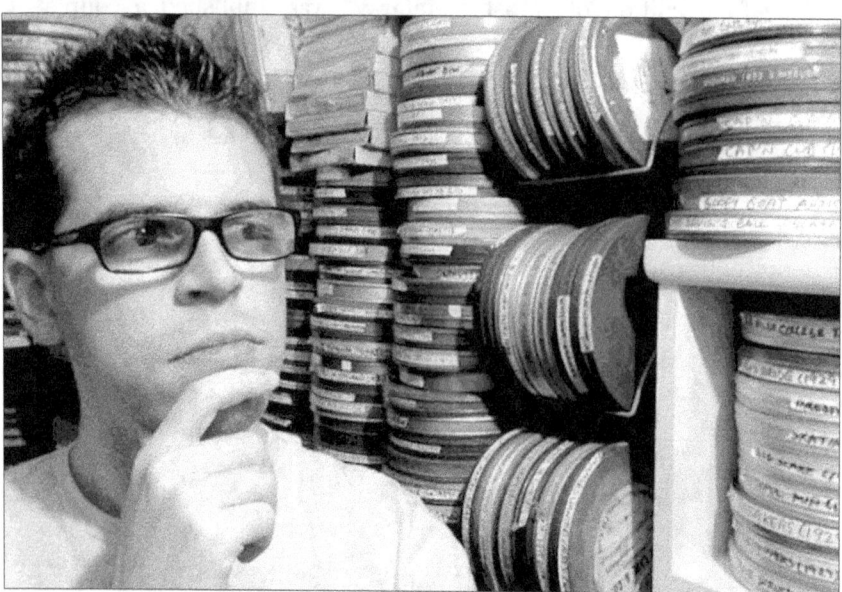

Animated film historian Tommy José Stathes.

"A selection of the 'Us Fellers' cartoons were subsequently reissued [by Bray] in 16mm film for home use in the 1940's, and some titles were also offered as air time slot filler material for early television use in the 1950's," Stathes stated. "Both instances gave Carlson an unlikely, albeit still limited spotlight for a few decades following his career in animation."

Carlson's works in the 1920's on an animated iteration of the popular "The Gumps" comic strip series also ensured his animation legacy included a notable association with a famous comic strip franchise, Stathes added.

While the discovery of every one of Carlson's "Dreamy Dud" cartoons has not materialized, many have been rescued and preserved through Stathe's efforts, with the assistance of other scholars, archivists, and collectors.

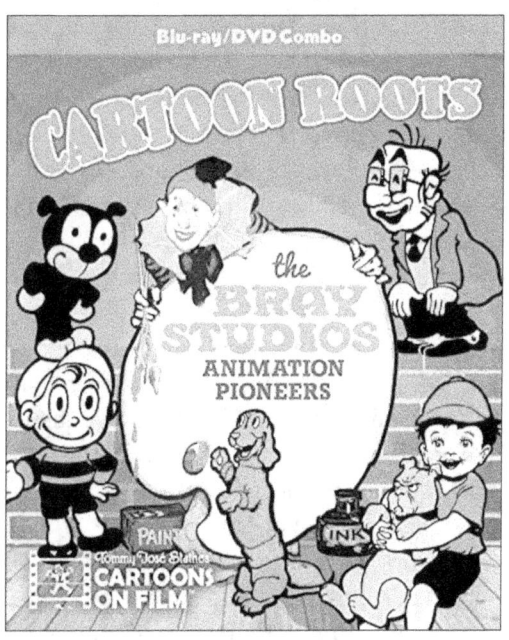

"Cartoon Roots: Bray Studios—Animation Pioneers."

"Among the couple dozen Essanay 'Dreamy Dud' and Bray 'Us Fellers' cartoons that were made featuring Dud, I estimate roughly a dozen of these films are currently known to survive in some form," Stathes said. "As far as Bray cartoons are concerned, there are long term plans in place to hopefully re-release more of the films held as part of my Bray Animation Project archives in the future."

Tommy José Stathes discovered a real Wallace A. Carlson cinematic gem when he stumbled upon "How Animated Cartoons Are Made," which subsequently was released for public consumption as part of a Bray animation collection in 2016, "Cartoon Roots: Bray Studios—Animation Pioneers." The title, released on Blu-ray and DVD showcasing films from the Stathes Collection, was co-produced by Thunderbean Animation.

"A few years ago, in the early 2010's, I became aware of a number of 28mm prints being sold by a couple of antique radio repairmen in the midwest," Stathes explained. "As it turned out, the gentlemen had come into a cache of over 200 28mm prints, all dating to the late 1910's through early 1920's, that were stored in a barn for decades."

Stathes said the films were subsequently sold in small groups on eBay, and many of the offerings included Bray cartoons.

"At one point, a listing for 'How Animated Cartoons Are Made' was posted. I was not previously aware that this film had even been produced but was extremely excited about it upon seeing some frame grabs, and I bid to win," Stathes recalled. "Needless to say, this film is now recognized as an important part of the Bray animation cannon, and I'm proud to have produced a new digital restoration of the film as part of the 'Cartoon Roots: Bray Studios—Animation Pioneers' release."

The Blue-ray and DVD have received critical acclaim in Amazon reviews, which sells the 2-hours amination collection for under $20.00.

A fan of animation since childhood, Stathes' work not only involves researching the history of early cartoons, but more important, collecting and archiving as many examples as possible. His efforts to rescue titles of early animated films and preserve them allows the public to enjoy and study these pioneering works. Stathes can always use a helping hand, both concerning locating and acquiring such films, and financial resources to make it possible.

"I work with film archives, private collectors, and other sources to make this possible, and have gradually developed multiple means to share these films with the public," he said.

Visit or contact Tommy José Stathes through his personal website: www.tommyjose.com.

We encourage everyone to discover the complete world of Bray and its animation history at brayanimation.weebly.com.

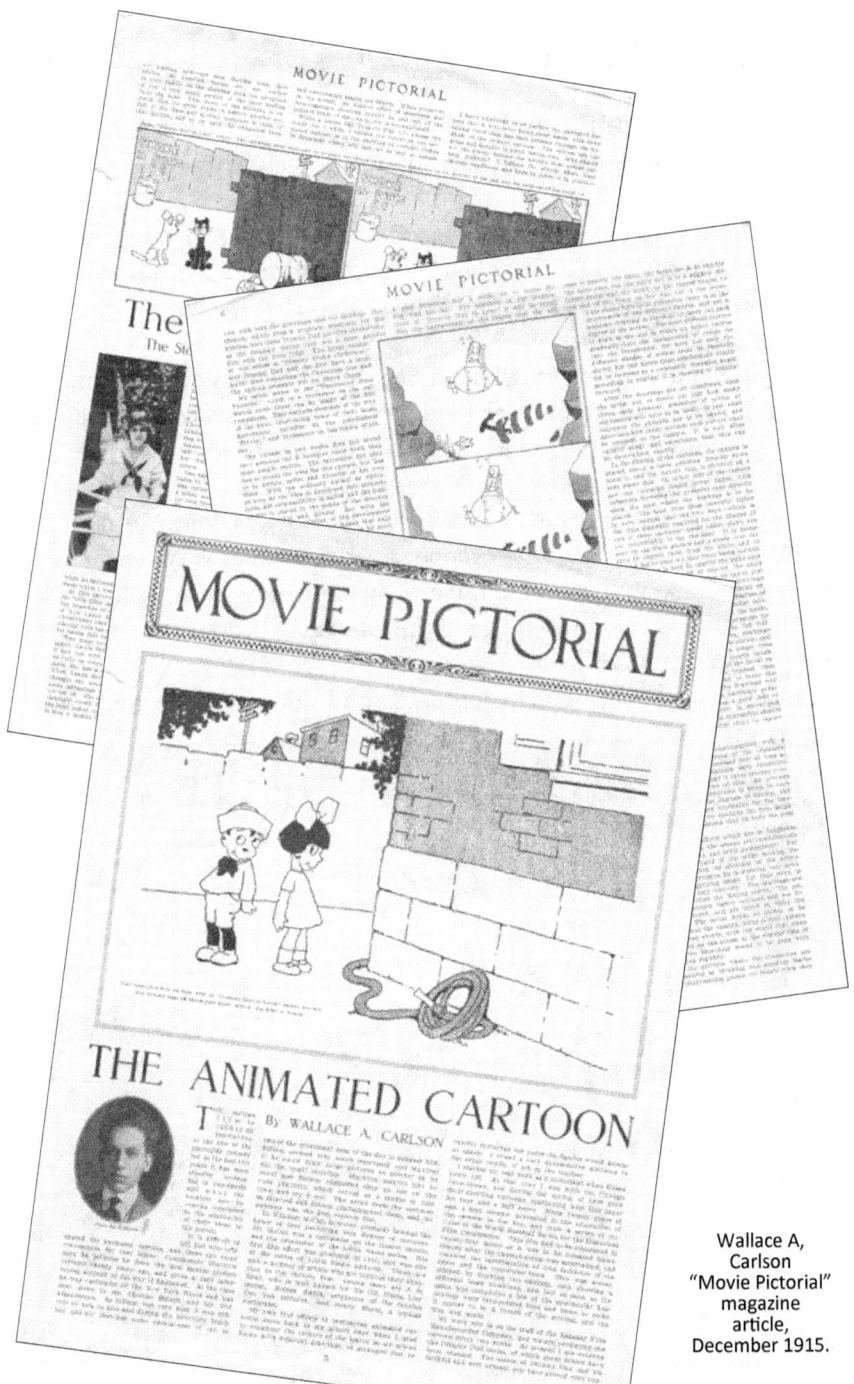

Wallace A, Carlson "Movie Pictorial" magazine article, December 1915.

THE ANIMATED CARTOON

From Movie Pictorial magazine, December 1915
Written by Wallace A. Carlson:

The cartoon film is rather an innovation in the line of the photoplay comedy but in the last two years has been steadily increasing in popularity, and many cartoonists are becoming interested in the adaptation of their ideas to the screen.

It is difficult to tell just who originated the animated cartoon, and there are many contestants for that honor. Commodore Blackton says he believes he drew the first motion picture cartoon twenty years ago and gave a very interesting account of the way it happened. At the time he was a cartoonist for the New York World and was sent down to see Thomas Edison and his kinetoscope. As Edison was very deaf, it was difficult to talk to him, and during the interview, Blackton quickly sketched some caricatures of one of the two of the prominent men of the day to interest him.

Edison seemed very much impressed and inquired if he could draw

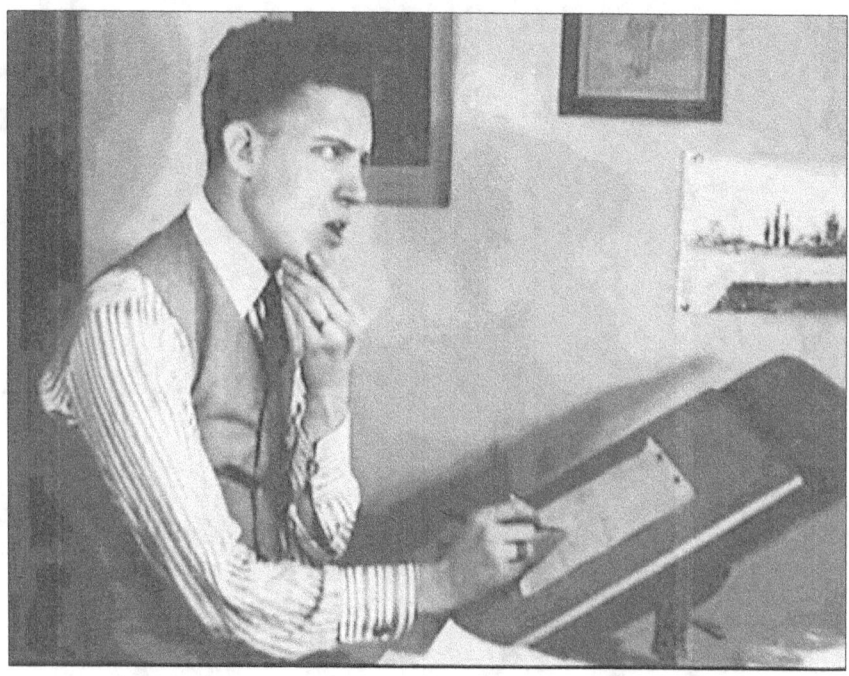

Carlson at the drawing board, 1919, Bray Animation Project/Stathes Collection.

14

large pictures as quickly as he did the small sketches. Blackton assured him he could, and Edison suggested they go out on the rude platform, which served as a studio at that time and try it out. The artist drew the cartoons as directed and Edison photographed them, and the outcome was the very first cartoon film.

To Winsor McCay, however, probably belongs the honor of first perfecting this filming of cartoons. Mr. McCay was a cartoonist for Hearst papers and the originator of the "Little Nemo" series. His first film effort was produced in 1910 and was one of the series of "Little Nemo" pictures.

There are now a number of artists who are turning their attention to the cartoon film; among them are J. R. Bray, who is well known for his "Col. Heeza Lair" series; Sidney Smith, the originator of the famous "Doc Yak" pictures; and Henry Meyer, a topical cartoonist.

My own first efforts in portraying animated cartoons date back to my school days when I used to ornament the corners of the leaves in my school books with different drawings, so arranged that by rapidly fluttering the pages the figures would appear to dance. I found a very appreciative audience in the other pupils, if not in the teacher.

I started my real work as a cartoonist when 15 years old. At the time I

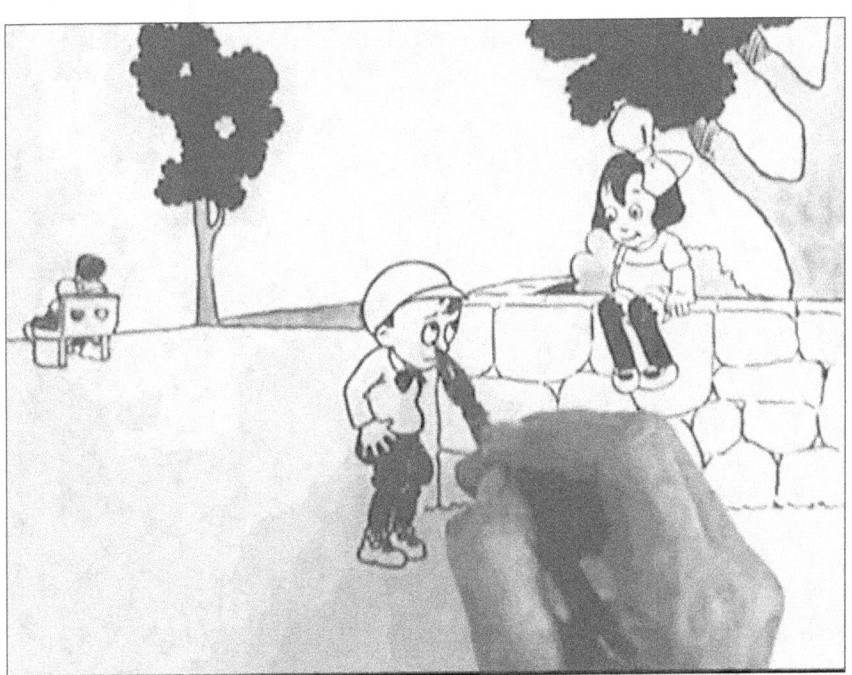

Carlson illustrating Dreamy Dud, 1919, Bray Animation Project/Stathes Collection.

was with the Chicago Inter-Ocean, and during the spring of 1909 drew their sporting cartoons, continuing with the paper for four and a half years. When 20 years of age, I became interested in the adaptation of the cartoon to film and drew a series of pictures of the World Baseball Series for the Historical Film Corporation. This film had to be completed in 24 hours as it was to be released immediately after the championship was ascertained, and required the incorporation of true incidents of the game and the victorious team. This was accomplished by drawing two endings, each showing a different team victorious, and just as soon as the game was completed a few of the spectator happenings were interpolated here and there to make it appear to be a record of the scoring, and the film was made.

My work is now on the staff of the Essanay Film Manufacturing Company, and we are producing one new cartoon every two weeks. At present, I am running the "Dreamy Dud" series, of which about fifteen [shorts] have been released. The antics of Dreamy Dud and his faithful and ever present pup have proved very popular with both the grown-ups and the children. One theater, which runs a program especially for the kiddies, uses these Dreamy Dud pictures extensively, as the manager claims they are the most popular film with the little folks. The latest re-

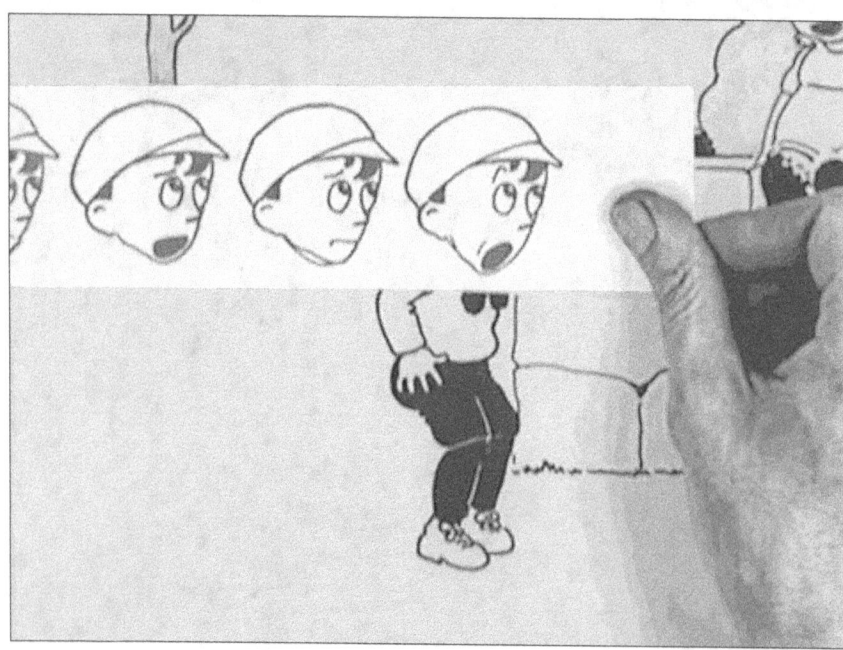

Carlson shows how to change the facial expressions on Dreamy Dud. Bray Animation Project/ Stathes Collection.

lease of this series is "Dreamy Dud's Christmas," and Dreamy Dud and the pup have a most joyful time inspecting the Christmas tree and the various presents left by Santa.

My latest series [is], "Canimated Nooz Pictorial," which is a burlesque on the animated news items run by many of the film companies. They include sketches of the hour, illustrating some of their latest movements; parodies on the joke-famous "flivver;" and burlesque on the topics of the day.

One release in two weeks does not sound very arduous, but it involves more work than most people realize. The cartoonist not only has to create the idea for the picture but has to be the author, artist, and director of his own films. With the ordinary author or editor, as soon as the idea is developed into scenario form, his responsibility is ended, and the manuscript is placed in the hands of the director for production and filming. But with the cartoonist and completion of the development of his idea in the drawings means that only half the work is completed, and now he must go into the studio and become the director, staying with his production every minute, instructing the cameraman, and personally attending to every detail of the filming.

The basic principles of the preparing of the cartoon comedy are very

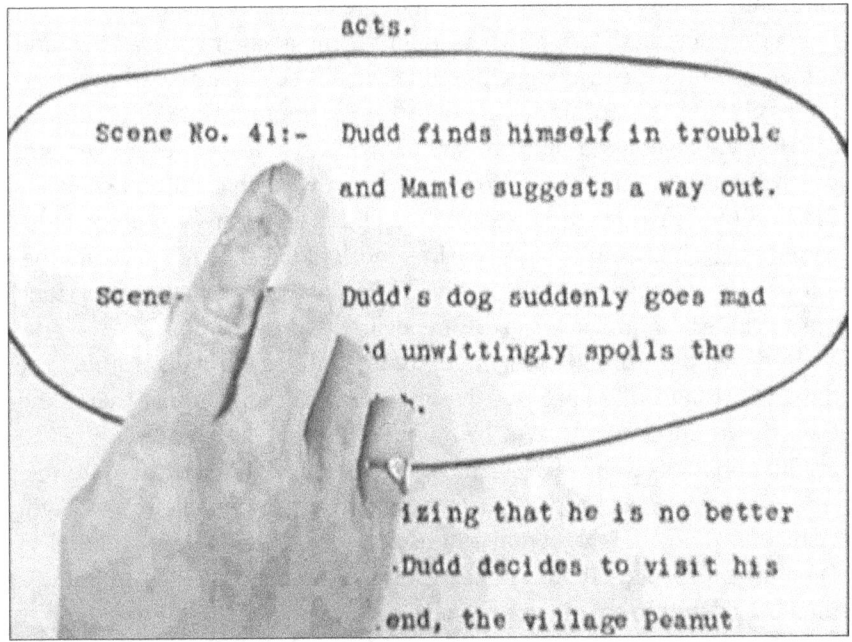

acts.

Scene No. 41:- Dudd finds himself in trouble
                and Mamie suggests a way out.

Scene   Dudd's dog suddenly goes mad
               'd unwittingly spoils the

               izing that he is no better
               ·Dudd decides to visit his
               .end, the village Peanut

Carlson points to scene instructions for a Dreamy Dud cartoon, 1919, Bray Animation Project/ Stathes Collection.

similar to those of writing a scenario. The first comes with the creation of an original idea, then the outline of the plot—if you could really say these comedies have plots—followed by the development of the action by a series of drawings corresponding to the action scenes in the scenario. The action in the cartoon also has to be explained by subtitles just as in a regular photoplay, and they must be carefully thought out.

The photo playwright thinks a great deal of work is entailed in developing a comedy into about 60 or 70 scenes, to fill one reel [of film], but in the cartoon comedy, it takes 1,200 to 1,500 drawings to fill a split-reel of five hundred feet. There is, generally, no written outline of the picture but the original idea is amplified and developed as the drawing progresses, and humor and comedy action are added. The comedy is easily injected by slick stick actions, as these are not objected to in the line drawings as they are in photoplays, and they always bring a laugh. The chasing and falling down of characters are very popular in these pictures, and the hard fall or the blow that causes the victim to see stars always appeals to the risibility [inclination to laugh]. The audience will break into an uproar over a dog chasing a cat in these drawings, whereas they probably would not even smile at the same action in a photoplay. The movements of all the figures are necessarily rather jerky and automatic, as this in itself adds much to the humor of the action.

Every moment shown on the screen means a separate drawing, and sometimes in these drawings, the difference is so slight that it is almost impossible for the uninitiated to detect it. In the first three illustrations of "Henry Flivver's Submarine," are shown three degrees of movement, you will have to study them closely to detect just what difference exists in the three drawings because it is so slight. The [deep sea] diver is depicted emerging from the submarine and looking through a periscope, but only by comparing his relative position as gauged by the periscope are you able to appreciate the difference in the poses.

In developing the idea in the cartoon film several backgrounds are drawn first, and these are printed and many copies made of them, and then the animation is drawn in by hand, step by step in the different graduations of action, each shade of movement making a separate picture. The figures are repeated in these backgrounds, and just a slight change is shown in the actual expression or a little angle in the tail of Dreamy Dud's pup. It may take several different drawings to show a man breaking into a smile, or to make the dog wag his tail. For example, in the illustrations of "Dreamy Dud in Love" it will be noted that the background of the fences and the ash cans is exactly the same, the large

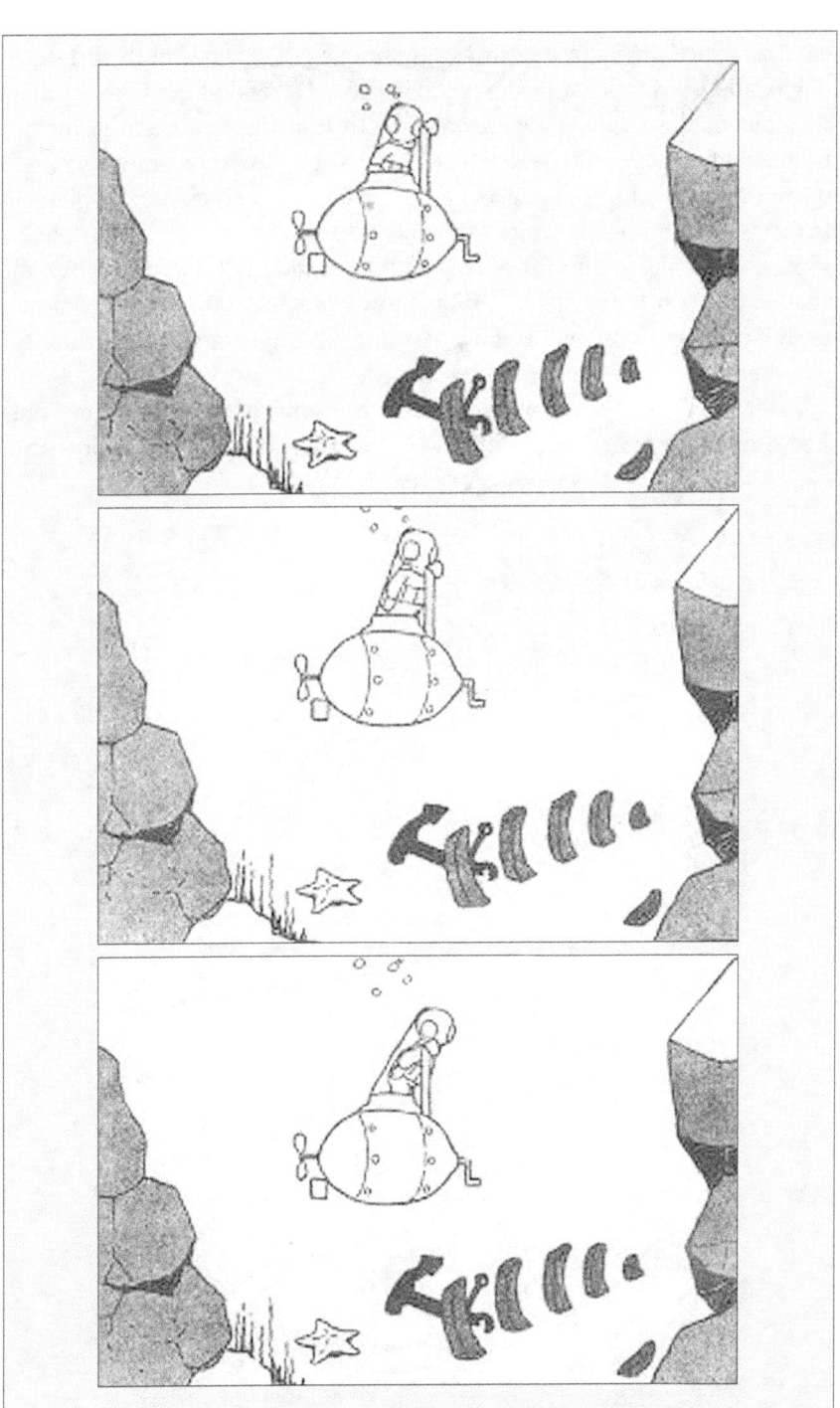

Succession of illustrations for Carlson's "Henry Flivver's Submarine" cartoon.

cat is in exactly the same pose, but the pup's tail is at a slightly different angle, and the small cat has moved nearer to the end of the fence on her way out of the scene. This shows how little difference there is in the movements of the different figures, and yet a separate drawing is required to carry out each degree of the action. The most difficult picture to draw is the one in which an object retires gradually in the background or comes up into the foreground, for here not only the different shades of action must be carefully shown but the figure must consistently diminish or increase at a constantly changing angle according to whether it is receding or coming forward.

After the drawings are all completed, then the artist has to figure out just how many times each different graduation of action or expression

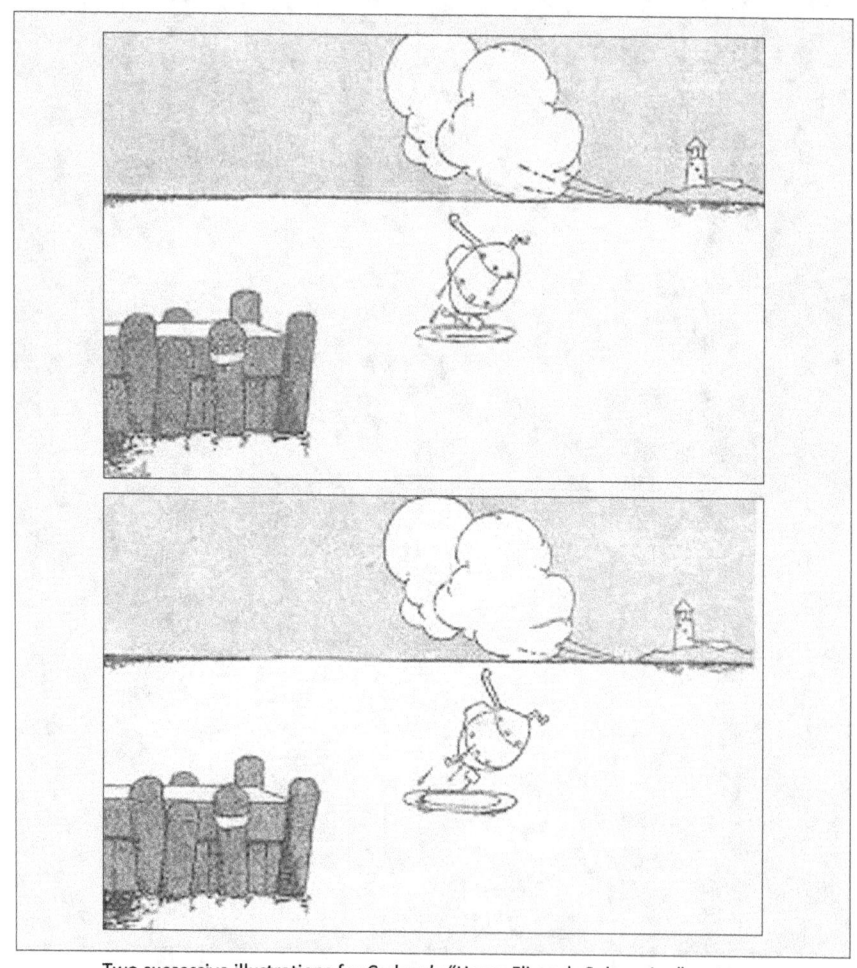

Two successive illustrations for Carlson's "Henry Flivver's Submarine" cartoon.

will have to be used; in just what sequence the pictures are to be shown, and ascertain how many seconds each picture shall be exposed to the camera. It is only after careful study and experience that this can be determined exactly.

In the filming of cartoons, the camera is placed above a table pointing directly down upon it, and the cameraman is elevated on a seat above this. On either side of the camera are one thousand candle power lights, with reflectors throwing the powerful rays directly upon the spot where the drawing is to be placed. The heat from these powerful lights is very intense, and the two days—which is the time generally required for filming one of these cartoons—spent under them, are not comfortable, to say the least. It is necessary to use black glasses and a shade over my eyes to protect them from the glare, and to wear a hat to keep my hair from being burned. Each drawing is held in exactly the same spot under the camera and at exactly the same angle. Each drawing may not be taken just once but many times. For example, drawings one to seven may be depicting the facial expressions undergone in the different degrees of a smile. Number one will be the somber face, number two the first sug-

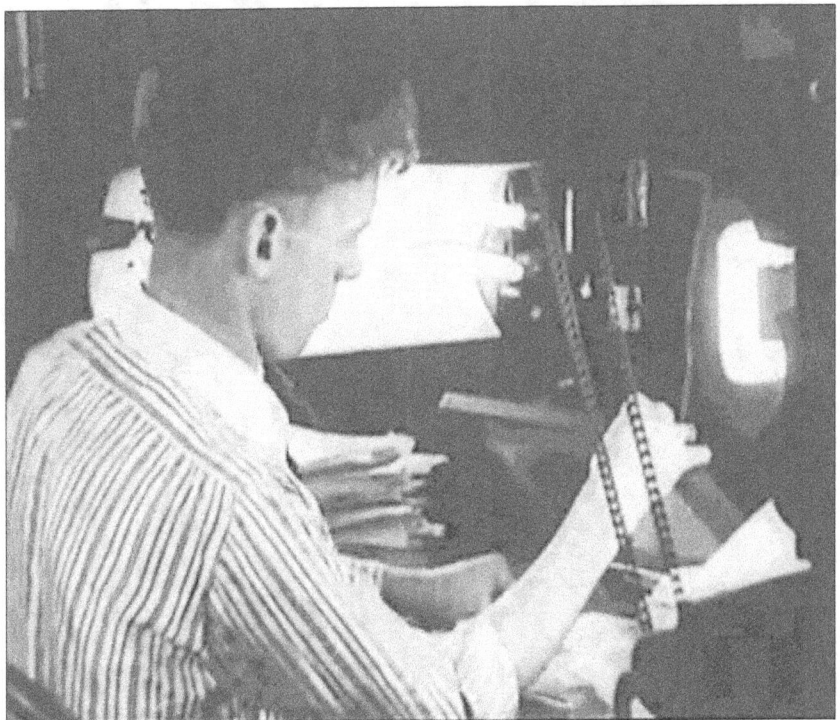

Carlson demonstrating the photography stage involving his illustrations. Bray Animation Project/ Stathes Collection.

gestion of a smile, and so by degrees, the smile will progress up to number seven, which may be the full grown laugh. Under the camera, drawings one to seven will be filmed consecutively, and number seven will be exposed a longer time than the others to show a hearty laugh. Then to produce the changing of the facial expression, number two will be exposed, then five, then three, then six. And to make the laugh gradually fade away the drawings will be reversed and exposed in backward order from seven to one. It takes a good deal of careful thought and practice to know just how long each graduation of expression should be exposed, and in just what order to expose the drawings.

The cartoons [drawings] are photographed with a "stop camera" instead of a cinematograph, and so can be exposed just as long as desired. With this camera, each revolution means one exposure, and it takes sixteen revolutions to make a foot of film. An average exposure of two revolutions is given to each drawing showing the degrees of motion, and four to sixteen exposures for the completed action (as for example the man laughing when it is desired that he hold the pose for a while).

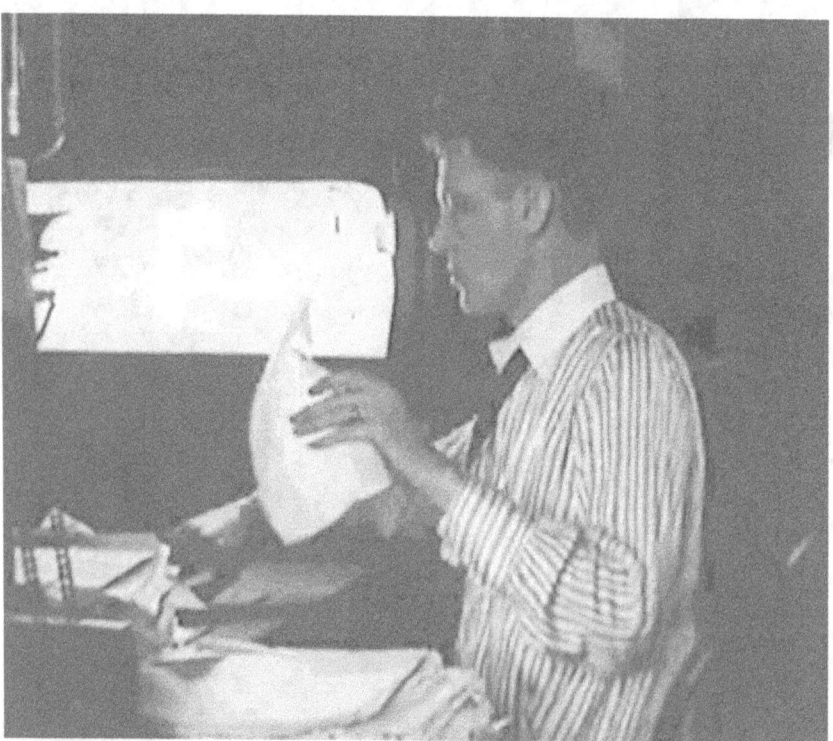

Carlson appears casual in this screenshot from "How Animated Cartoons Are Made," but stated the intensity of the lights required for filming caused him to wear black spectacles to reduce glare, and a hat to prevent his hair from being burned. Bray Animation Project/Stathes Collection.

Some of the effects which are so laughable and puzzling on the screen are combinations of trick drawing or trick photography. For instance, the hand of the artist holding the pen and making the sketches on the screen gives the impression he is drawing very accurately at lightning speed, but this work is really done very leisurely. The drawings are all made before the filming starts. The pictures are simply lightly outlined and not finished, however, and are inked under the camera. The artist works as slowly as he desires, and the camera, being a stop camera, is revolved slowly, with the result that when projected on the screen at the regular rate of speed the sketching seems to be done with lightning rapidity.

In the pictures where the characters are represented as thinking and question marks and interrogation points—or hearts when they are making love—are seen darting from their brains, the question marks, etc., are worked in very lightly on the drawing with the exception of just a very small portion of the lines leading away from the head. This much of the drawing is exposed, then the artist draws in heavily another section of the lines and another exposure is made of that portion, and so on until the completed lines and punctuation marks are drawn. When projected on the screen, the desired effect of the questions and interrogations shooting rapidly in and out of the puzzled brain of the characters is accomplished.

While a series like Dreamy Dud will please the public for a while, I believe the future of the animated cartoon is in the showing of current events by drawings which will instruct as well as amuse.

I have ambitions to so perfect the animated cartoon that it will drive home great issues with more telling force than has been possible through the medium of the printed cartoon. The movies are too great and durable to admit limitations. Why should not the screen become the world's most potent cartoon medium? I believe the screen offers ideal conditions and hope to prove it in practice.

DREAMY DUD
EPISODE GUIDE

The following episode descriptions are reprinted from magazine articles or film reviews from the time period, and/or IMDb descriptions, to ensure authenticity and minimize interpretation. Episodes without a synopsis are either in private collections with no storyline presented publicly, or due to the titles being undiscovered or noted as "lost films."

Dreamy Dud: An Alley Romance
Released May 15, 1915

Wag steals a hat and cane. He meets Miss Cat in an alley and flirts with her. Just as the two are spooning on a log, along comes Mr. Cat and chases Wag. Dreamy Dud tries to save him and runs after him. He trees Mr. Cat and shakes the tree, whereupon Mr. Cat descends on his head and is administering a beating when Dreamy Dud wakes up to find his mother pulling his hair.

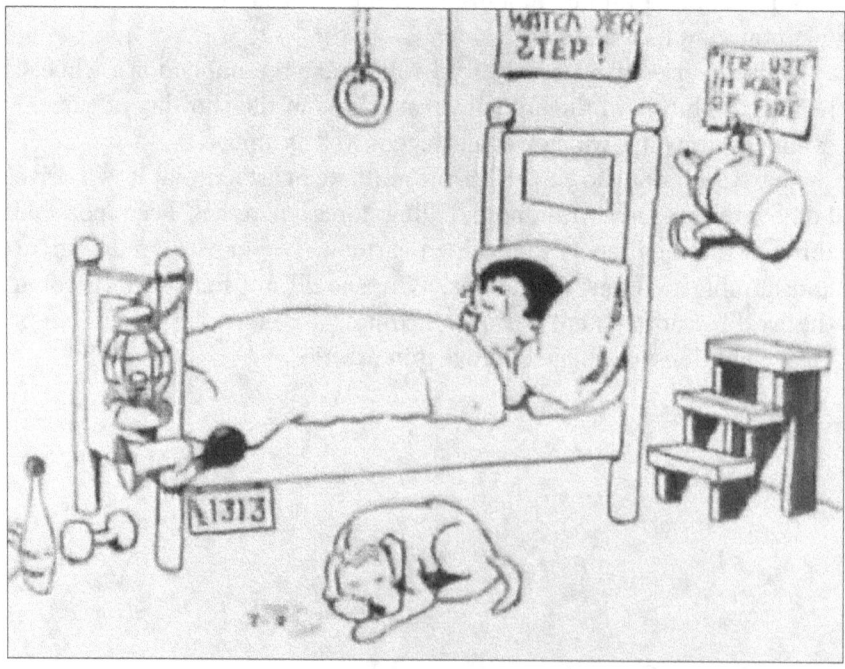

Dreamy Dud in his bedroom with loyal dog Wags.

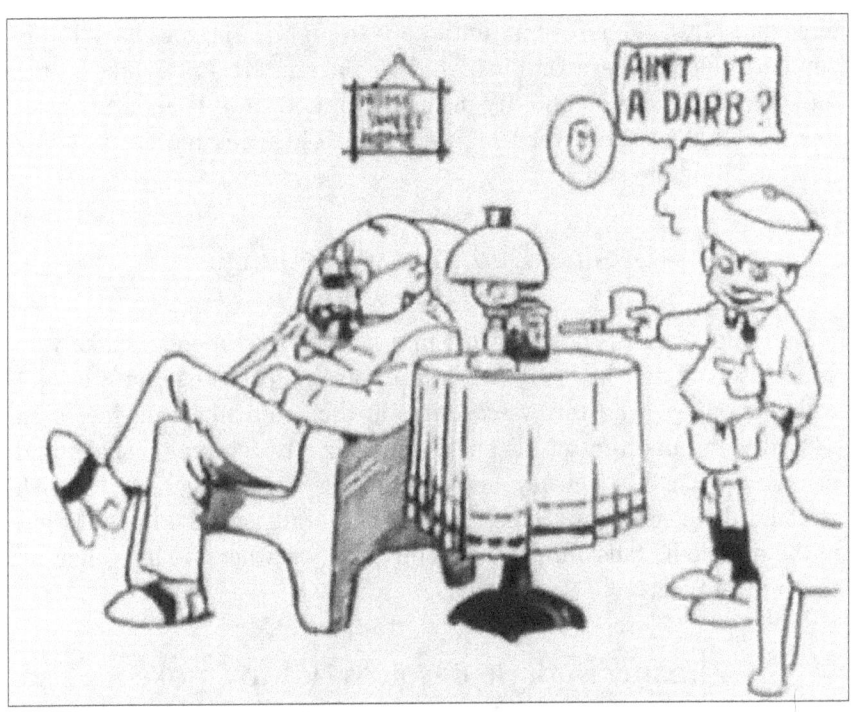

"Dreamy Dud: He Resolves Not to Smoke," 1915.

Dreamy Dud: And a Visit to the Zoo

Released May 26, 1915

Dreamy Dud and Wag, his dog, while out on a lark, make a visit to the Zoo, but the monkey beats them both up, the elephant gets peeved when Wag bites his tail and throws Wag into the lagoon and squirts water all over Dud. The kangaroo chases them both clear out of the picture, just as Dud's mother calls him for the forty-eleventh time.

Dreamy Dud: In the Swim

Released June 7, 1915

Dud and Wag, his dog, eat too much jam and at once swell up to enormous size, just as Dud's mother told him he would if they stole jam. They shrink just as quickly and become so small that Dud can just look over the top of a tea cup, filled with milk and standing in a saucer. Dud balances on the edge of the cup and does high dives, as does Wag. They tire of this just as Mr. Cat comes along. Dud climbs down on the floor, where Mr. Cat plays with him as it would with a ball of yarn, incidentally giving Dud a "ride a cock horse to Banbury Cross" on its tail. Wag interferes and Mr. Cat chases him until he is tired. Mr. Cat goes back to the cup and saucer, where Dud is high diving again. Mr. Cat drinks all the milk leaving Dud high and dry in the bottom. Mr. Cat is about to swallow the terrified Dud, when he wakes up to hear his mother scolding him for eating the jam.

Dreamy Dud: Lost in the Jungle
Released June 9, 1915

Dud and Wag, his dog, get lost in a jungle. They meet a snake who swallows Wag and has to cough him up again. Then they have a fight with a monkey, who throws coconuts at them. Finally, Dud meets an ostrich who puts him on his back. Then Mr. Ostrich sees a snake and runs away. On his journey he comes upon a precipice. Mr. Ostrich stretches his neck clear across. Dud starts to walk across on it, but right in the middle he falls and wakes up on the floor, where he has fallen on the faithful Wag.

Dreamy Dud: He Resolves Not to Smoke
Released June 22, 1915

Dreamy Dud commands his dog Wag to do a few tricks. The charming canine happily performs them, plus Dud and Wag, his dog, always looking for mischief, find Dud's father's pipe and the pipe is strong. Dud

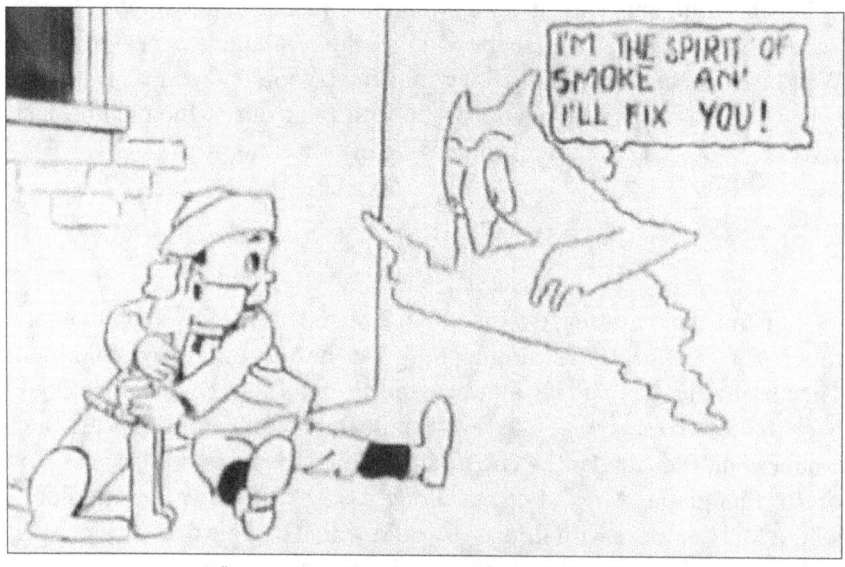

"Dreamy Dud: He Resolves Not to Smoke," 1915.

26

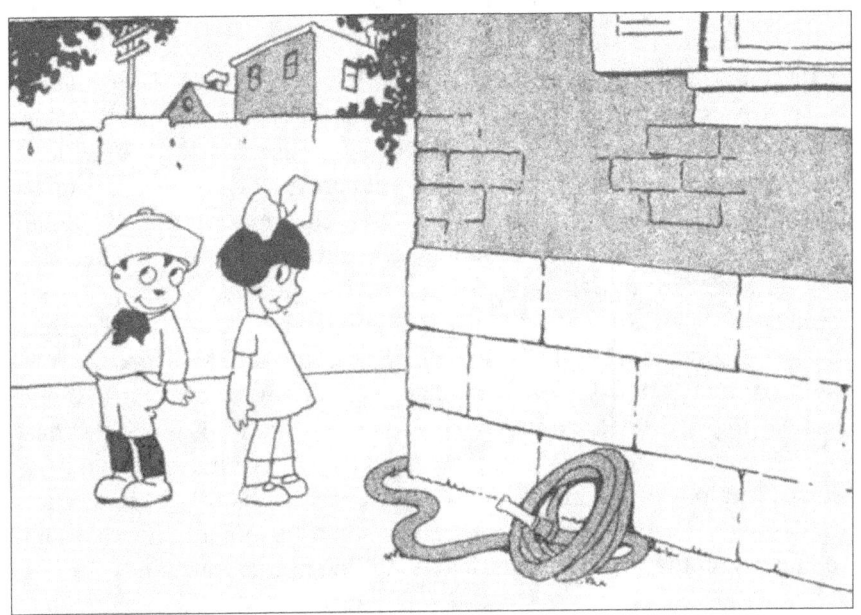

"Dreamy Dud in Love," 1915.

resolves to smoke. He does so with dire consequences. The Spirit of Smoke appears and carries Dud away into the clouds, far above the stars, and leaves him hanging on a corner of the moon. Wag weeps so many tears that he forms a lake and drowns himself. Dud tells the moon a funny story and gets dumped off into space for his pains, because of the moon's boisterous laughter. Dud falls and falls and falls. He wakes up on the floor of his bedroom and declared to Wag that he will never smoke again. The children will scream with delight when they see this picture and the older folks will laugh until they cry.

Dreamy Dud: King Coo Koo's Kingdom
Released July 7, 1915

Dud and Wag, his dog, go on a visit to Africa, where Dud is captured by some natives. He pleases the king so much that he steps down from the throne and gives it to Dud. They do everything possible to please him. Ballet girls dance for him and musicians thrum their instruments. Finally he is offered the choice of all the dusky ladies of the kingdom as a wife. He refuses to choose any of them, and even laughs at their oddity. This displeases the people, and he is dethroned and put into a kettle to be boiled for dinner. Then Dud wakes up.

Dreamy Dud: He Goes Bear Hunting
Released July 28, 1915

Dreamy Dud is fingering his rifle and telling Wag what a great shot he is. He aims over his shoulder and shoots his initials in the board fence. He aims at a crow in a tree, but cannot kill it because the crow ducks each time he shoots and then eats the bullets as they are shot. Finally Dud gives up and determines to kill a bear. He and Wag tramp off and discover a Teddy bear which Dud chases and is about to kill when the mother bear runs out and chases Dud. He is frightened and runs into a tree. Down below the mother bear is raging and shaking the tree. Dud drops the gun and the bear picks it up, squints into the muzzle and, pulling the trigger, killing herself. Then the old father bear hurries out and, seeing the dead mother bear, becomes wrathful and questions Dud, who is terrified in the tree still. Dud won't say much and the bear shakes him out to the ground. Dud runs away and is caught in a fence when the bear catches up to him. The bear shakes him and he wakes up to find his mother bending over his bed telling him to wake up.

Dreamy Dud: A Visit to Uncle Dudley's Farm
Released August 4, 1915

Dreamy Dud and Wag, the dog, are given the freedom of their uncle's great farm and so set out to investigate the barnyard. First they run into the stable where the horses are munching. Wag is interested in the

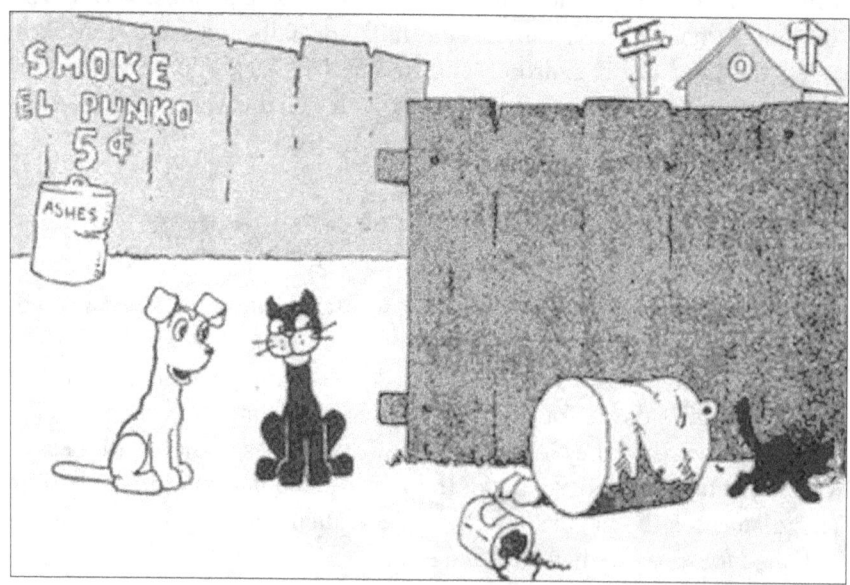

"Dreamy Dud in Love," 1915.

chickens and succeeds in getting into a fight with a rooster, when he teased a hen who was pulling a worm out of the ground. While Wag is fighting joyously with the rooster, Dud is being picked up by the seat of the trousers by the horse and thrown high into the air. He comes down near the cow and is hooked high in the air. When he comes down he alights on the calf and promptly endeavors to ride the little animal about the pasture. When the bull sees him he tosses him to the cow. The bull and cow toss Dud back and forth and finally Dud is thrown high into the air and into the belfry of a church steeple, where his body rings the bell. This wakes him up and he jumps out of the bed to stop the alarm clock.

Dreamy Dud: Cowboy
Released September 15, 1915

Dreamy Dud, gazing at a bill poster announcing the coming of a Wild West Show, enthuses over the lot of the cowboy, and informs Wag, his dog, that the "blooey, blooey" life is the real thing. Forthwith Wag is transformed into a blooded steed, and Dud's commonplace "duds" give way to a regulation "Bronco Billy" outfit. Dud's steed races over hill and

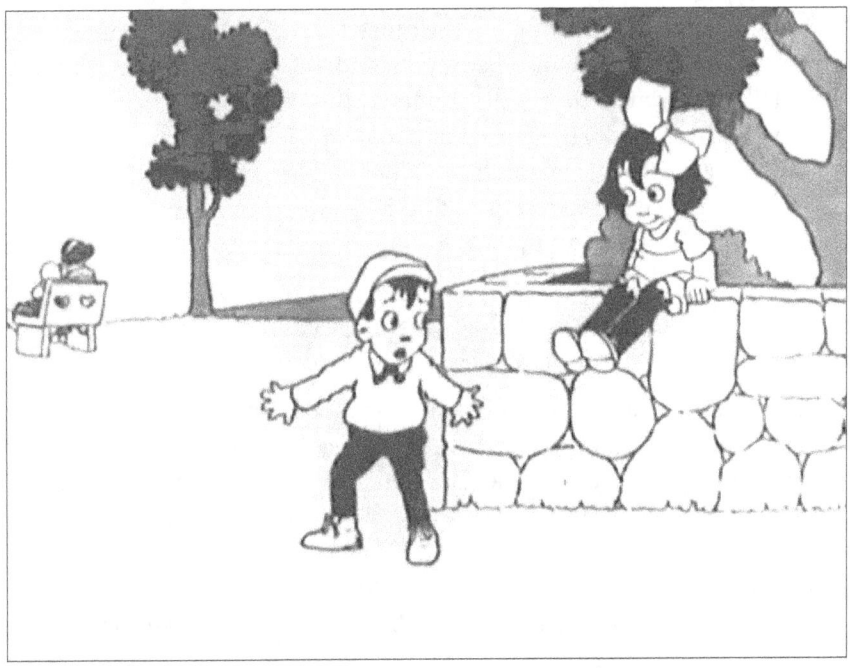

Dreamy Dud appearance in "How Animated Cartoons are Made," 1919, Bray Animation Project/ Stathes Collection.

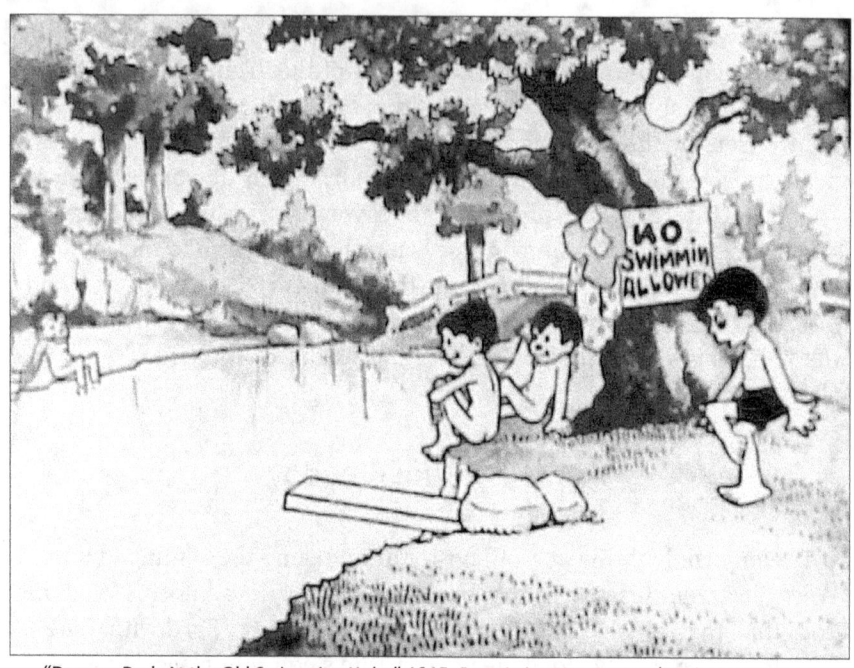

"Dreamy Dud: At the Old Swimming Hole," 1915, Bray Animation Project/Stathes Collection.

dale, leaping lofty crags like a mountain goat. Suddenly Dud finds himself on the edge of a canyon. On the other side a fair damsel bound to a tree is about to be tomahawked by an Indian. Dud lassos the Indian, who falls apparently to his death, down the canyon. Dud crosses the canyon on his lariat. The damsel is freed, and she is kissing him, when the Indian pops up from behind a boulder and is just shaking the life out of Dud, when Dreamy awakens to find his mother standing over his bed, telling him it's time to get up.

Dreamy Dud: Dud at the Old Swimming Hole
Released September 29, 1915

Dreamy Dud takes a swim in the river. He is chased by a turtle but manages to escape its clutches. Later he dives to the bottom of the river, where he sees a beautiful mermaid. He is very much frightened by a watchdog fish's loud barking, but after a desperate encounter, worsens it. Dreamy then expresses love to the mermaid and shows her all the tricks in which he is expert. She is so delighted that she kisses him. Dreamy is transported to the seventh heaven, when he wakes up to find it was too good to be true.

Dreamy Dud: Sees Charlie Chaplin
Released October 27, 1915

Dreamy Dud and his dog, Wag, are down-hearted because they haven't the money to go into a movie theater and see a Chaplin picture. A dime rolls out of the theater, which someone has dropped, and Dud picks it up. In the theater they see Chaplin fighting with a donkey. When he flirts with a girl whose back is toward him, a policeman tries to arrest him. The donkey and the policeman collide and exchange kicks. Chaplin laughs when the policeman is kicked over. Then the donkey kicks Chaplin and he flies into the air and lands in a lake. Dud wakes up and finds his father bending over him asking what he is dreaming about.

Dreamy Dud: In Love
Released December 8, 1915

Dreamy Dud sees his dog, Wag, expressing love to a cat and is congratulating himself on not being susceptible to the charms of the fair sex, when he spies a little girl making eyes at him. Dreamy Dud is not long in reaching her side and soon is in love with her. He is sitting on a box singing lullabies to her dolls, when he is awakened by his father who compliments him on his extremely fine voice.

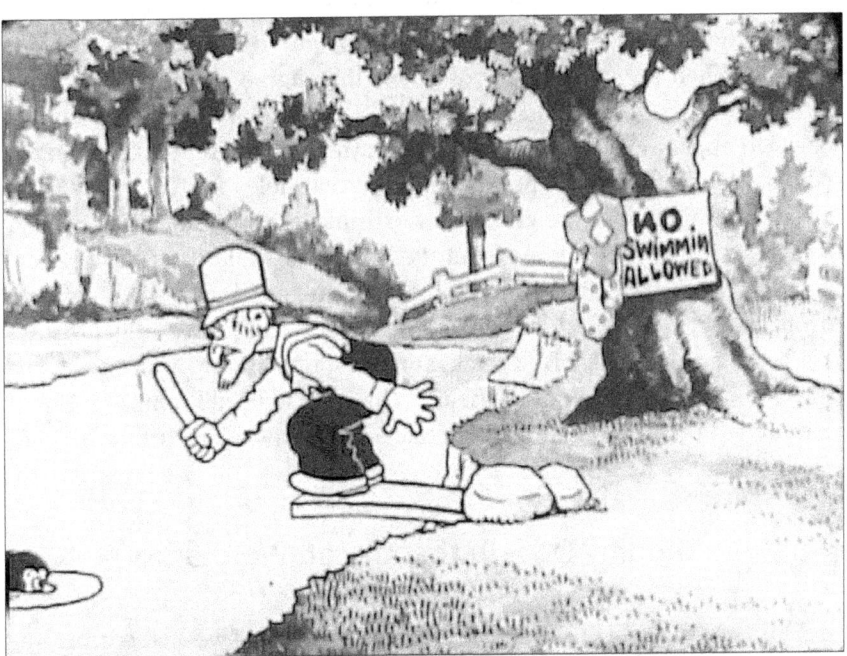

"Dreamy Dud: At the Old Swimming Hole," 1915, Bray Animation Project/Stathes Collection.

31

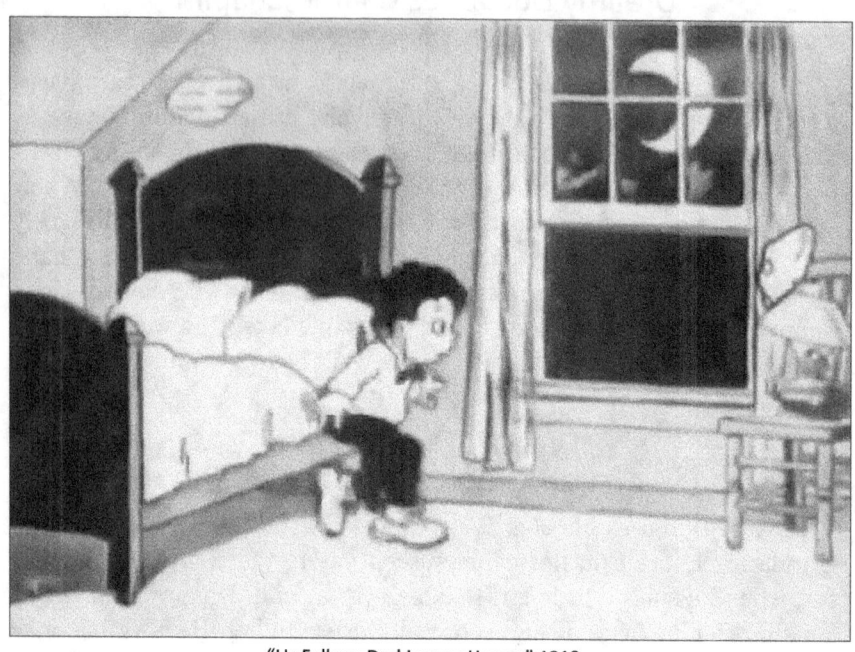

"Us Fellers: Dud Leaves Home," 1919.

Dreamy Dud: Lost at Sea
Released February 2, 1916

Dreamy Dud and his dog, Wag, go for a spin in the good motorboat, "Wow." When they are miles out at sea the engine stops. Dreamy Dud attempts to fix it, but has no success. Soon all sorts of sea monsters begin to appear around the boat. Finally the little vessel is sunk when a whole school of sawfish appear and saw great holes in it. Dreamy Dud, after swimming all day, sights what he thinks is an island. After finding refuge on it, he discovers he is on the back of a whale. He is finally rescued by an eagle that swoops down and carries him away. The eagle drops him on an island inhabited by cannibals. A big fat cannibal throws his boomerang at Dud. Dud ducks, the weapon, circling around, strikes the cannibal in the back of the head. When he falls, Dud jumps on top of him and is pounding him on the face when he awakens to find himself madly hammering his pillow.

Dreamy Dud: In the African War Zone
Released February 2, 1916

This is a split reel in which Cartoonist Carlson has worked out his humorous incidents by combining, through excellent double exposure, his human figures with his well-known pen and ink characters. Dreamy Dud, Dunk and the dog put out to sea. The captain orders the cook to quit boiling cabbage. The cook produces an alibi and Dunk's cigar is found to be the offensive smell. Before the captain can finish his argument a battleship opens fire on them, the gunners having orders to get the big fellow. Dud and the dog delight in Dunk's dodging of fourteen-inch shells. Then a gigantic whale lifts the three off the boat and sends them whirling into space. Dud comes down right through a newspaper in which a cannibal chieftain is reading the latest movie news. "Spoila pictura Hank Walthall," says the chief angrily. Dud is chased over the desert and caught, but the chief's daughter pleads for his life. He awakens to find the black washerwoman telling him to get up, while Dunk and the dog laugh.

Canimated Nooz Pictorial No. 15: Dreamy Dud
Released September 6, 1916

Dreamy Dud tries a trip in a submarine and blocks all the traffic on the ocean.

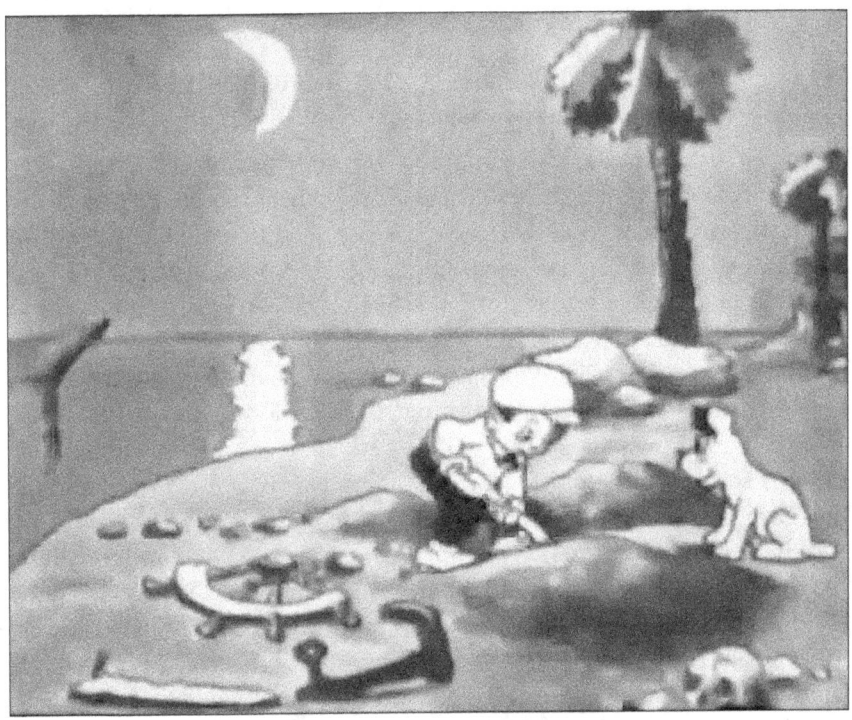

"Us Fellers: Dud Leaves Home," 1919.

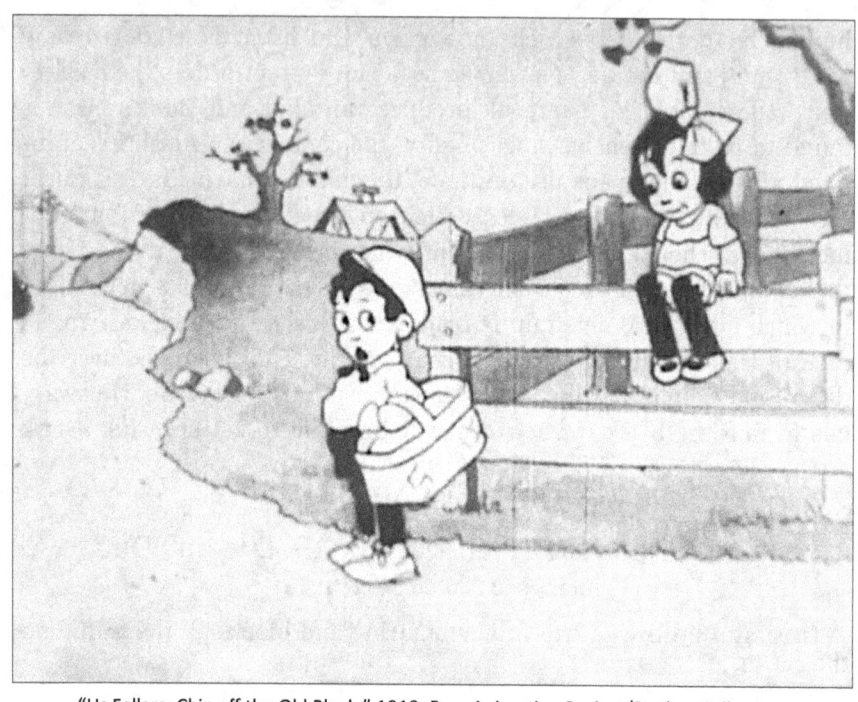
"Us Fellers: Chip off the Old Block," 1919, Bray Animation Project/Stathes Collection.

Dreamy Dud: Has a Laugh on the Boss
Released September 27, 1916

Novel trick photography combining the activities of living and pen-sketched subjects mark this split reel. Cartoonist Carlson goes to sleep at his drawing board as soon as he has sketched his familiar figures of Dreamy Dud and his dog Wag. Catching their boss asleep these two mischievous youngsters leap off the board and are off for some fun. They get into an apple orchard.

The farmer, Harry Dunkinson, is reading a "Diamond Dick" between blood-curdling interruptions by his parrot. He spies the trespassers, and with a blunderbuss fires at them. They retaliate so rapidly with apples that he shakes off the mortal coil and becomes an angel. What matter if his garb is a sheet, and his wings merely panama fans? Ascending, he reaches the moon and a wing breaks. A sign tells him it is only 983,000,000 miles to heaven, so he is discouraged. Spying Dreamy Dud in the orchard, he hurls a boot at him from the moon. He topples out of the tree. Carlson wakes up on the floor where he has fallen, to find Dreamy Dud, Wag, and Farmer Dunkinson all laughing at him. It was his own dream.

Dreamy Dud: Joyriding with Princess Zlim
Released November 29, 1916

Dreamy Dud finds himself in Africa, the reluctant escort of Princess Zlim, the ebony lady of pronounced pulchritude. She invites him to take a ride in the Royal Jitney Bus and after cranking the elephant's tail, they climb aboard. Gasoline is taken on for the elephant and after drinking it he becomes unsteady and engages in various fights with other animals, making it extremely hard for the Princess to make love to Dreamy Dud. The resultant adventures give Dud a thrilling time, but be soon wakes up to find his mother calling him.

Us Fellers: Dud Leaves Home
Released July 9, 1919

Dud's girlfriend Mamie wants an ice cream cone, but Dud is broke. He rushes home, steals a coin bank and chops it open with an ax, only to find that he's also split in half the one coin inside. Dud's mother sees this and spanks him. That night, Dud takes his dog and runs away into the woods. He imagines his mother finding him the next morning, weeping and reproaching herself for being so hard on him. Then he imagines finding buried treasure. These fantasies become nightmarish

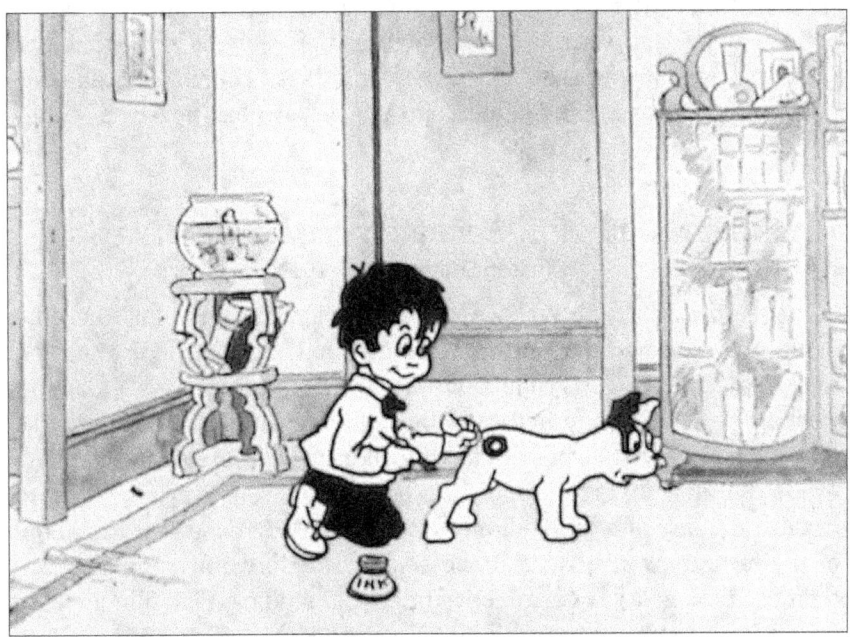

"Us Fellers: Dud's Haircut," 1920, Bray Animation Project/Stathes Collection.

35

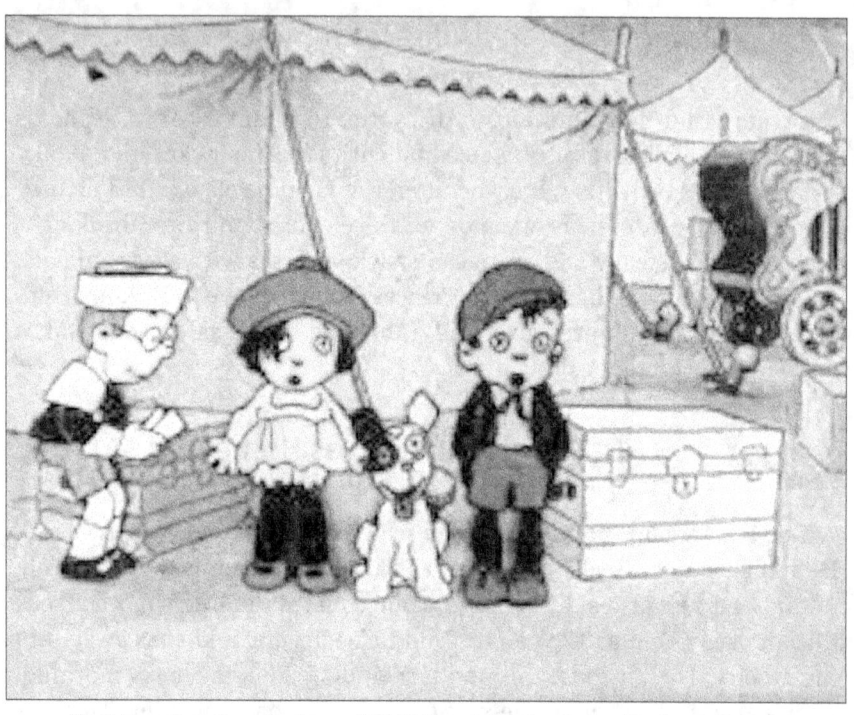

"Us Fellers: Dud, Circus Performer," 1919, Bray Animation Project/Stathes Collection.

when he thinks he sees a bear, a demon and a laughing skull. It's morning now, and Dud returns home with his dog, only to suffer another spanking from his mother. The dog says, "Guess I might as well start training for what's coming to me," and hits his own behind several times on a fence.

Dreamy Dud: How Animated Cartoons are Made
Released September 6, 1919

Pioneering animator Wallace A. Carlson stars in this film where he demonstrates how he creates a "Dreamy Dud" animated cartoon and photographs it at Bray Productions studio. In this film, we see Carlson working at his desk and taking us through the early animation process in a documentary-style presentation, exploring how cartoons were made over a century ago. Bray Productions founder John R. Bray also appears in this rare, one-of-a-kind, glimpse at Wallace A. Carlson at work. Many of the techniques displayed became early standards on animated cartoon production that were practiced by other studios. This film appears on "Cartoon Roots: Bray Studios—Animation Pioneers" on DVD.

Additional "Dreamy Dud" Titles
Released 1919-1920

The following "Dreamy Dud" adventures descriptions were unavailable. The titles alone provide a good indication of what they were about. "Dreamy Dud: Up in the Air," released October 27, 1915. "Dreamy Dud: The Circus Performer," released May 14, 1919. "Dreamy Dud: Home Run," released September 23, 1919. "Dreamy Dud: Geography Lesson," released November 17, 1919. "Dreamy Dud: Chip Off the Old Block," released December 31, 1919. "Dreamy Dud: Dud's Haircut," released February 16, 1920. "Dreamy Dud: Lion Tamer," released September 9, 1920.

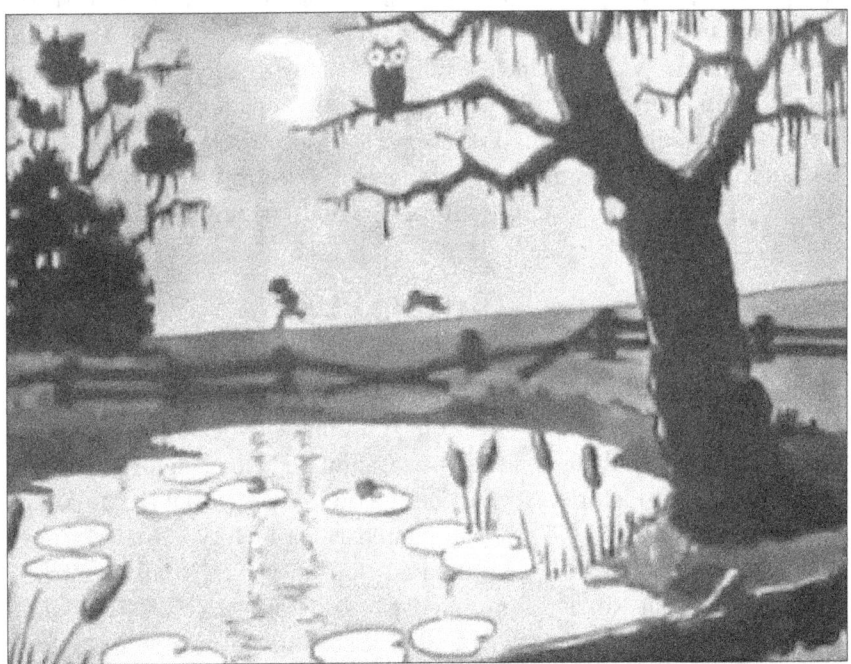

Carlson's background art in later "Dreamy Dud" cartoons featured amazing detail and use of shadows and reflective light, such as this example from "Us Fellers: Dud Leaves Home," 1919.

WALLACE A. CARLSON FILMOGRAPHY

1914 Films

Introducing Charlie Chaplin, Joe Boko Breaking Into the Big League.

1915 Films

Canimated Nooz Pictorial No. 1, Dreamy Dud in Love, Canimated Nooz Pictorial No. 2, Dreamy Dud in the Air, Canimated Nooz Pictorial No. 3, Dreamy Dud at the Old Swimmin' Hole, Dreamy Dud Cowboy, Joe Boko in Saved by Gasoline, Dreamy Dud Sees Charlie Chaplin, Dreamy Dud: A Visit to Uncle Dudley's Farm, Dreamy Dud: He Goes Bear Hunting, Dreamy Dud in King Koo Koo's Kingdom, Dreamy Dud: He Resolves Not to Smoke, Joe Boko in a Close Shave, Dreamy Dud: Lost in the Jungle, Dreamy Dud in the Swim, Dreamy Dud and a Visit to the Zoo, Dreamy Dud: An Alley Romance and Dreamy Dud: A Visit to the Zoo.

1916 Films

Canimated Nooz Pictorial No. 6, Dreamy Dud Joyriding with Princess Zlim, Canimated Nooz Pictorial No. 7, Canimated Nooz Pictorial No. 8, Dreamy Dud in the African War Zone, Canimated Nooz Pictorial No. 9, Dreamy Dud Has a Laugh on the Boss, Canimated Nooz Pictorial No. 10, Canimated Nooz Pictorial No. 11, Canimated Nooz Pictorial No. 12, Canimated Nooz Pictorial No. 13, Canimated Nooz Pictorial No. 14, Canimated Nooz Pictorial No. 15, Canimated Nooz Pictorial No. 16, Canimated Nooz Pictorial No. 17, Canimated Nooz Pictorial No. 18, Joe Boko, Canimated Nooz Pictorial No. 19, Joe Boko's Adventures and Dreamy Dud Lost at Sea, Canimated Nooz Pictorial No. 20, Canimated Nooz Pictorial No. 21

1917 Films

Goodrich Dirt and the $1000 Reward, Goodrich Dirt's Amateur Night, Goodrich Dirt at the Training Camp, Goodrich Dirt Lunch Detective, Goodrich Dirt at the Seashore, Otto Luck and the Ruby of Razmataz, Otto Luck to the Rescue, Otto Luck in the Movies, Otto Luck's Flivvered Romance, Canimated Nooz Pictorial No. 22, Canimated Nooz Pictorial No. 23, Canimated Nooz Pictorial No. 24, Canimated Nooz Pictorial No. 25, Canimated Nooz Pictorial No. 26, Canimated Nooz Pictorial No. 27, Canimated Nooz Pictorial No. 28.

1918 Films

Goodrich Dirt in Spot Goes Romeoing, Goodrich Dirt Cow Puncher, Goodrich Dirt in When Wishes Come True, Goodrich Dirt Millionaire, Goodrich Dirt Coin Collector, Goodrich Dirt in the Dark and Stormy Night, Goodrich Dirt the Cop, Goodrich Dirt King of Spades, Goodrich Dirt in Darkest Africa, Goodrich Dirt the Bad-man Tamer, Goodrich Dirt Mat Artist, Goodrich Dirt in the Barber Business, Goodrich Dirt's Bear Hunt, Goodrich Dirt and the Duke de Whatanob.

1919 Films

Chip Off the Old Block, Dud's Geography Lesson, US Fellers: Dud Leaves Home, Dud's Home Run, How Animated Cartoons Are Made, Ol' Swimmin' Hole, Dud's Greatest Circus on Earth, Dud the Circus Performer, Wounded by the Beauty, The Parson, Dud Perkins Gets Mortified, Goodrich Dirt Hypnotist and Goodrich Dirt in a Difficult Delivery.

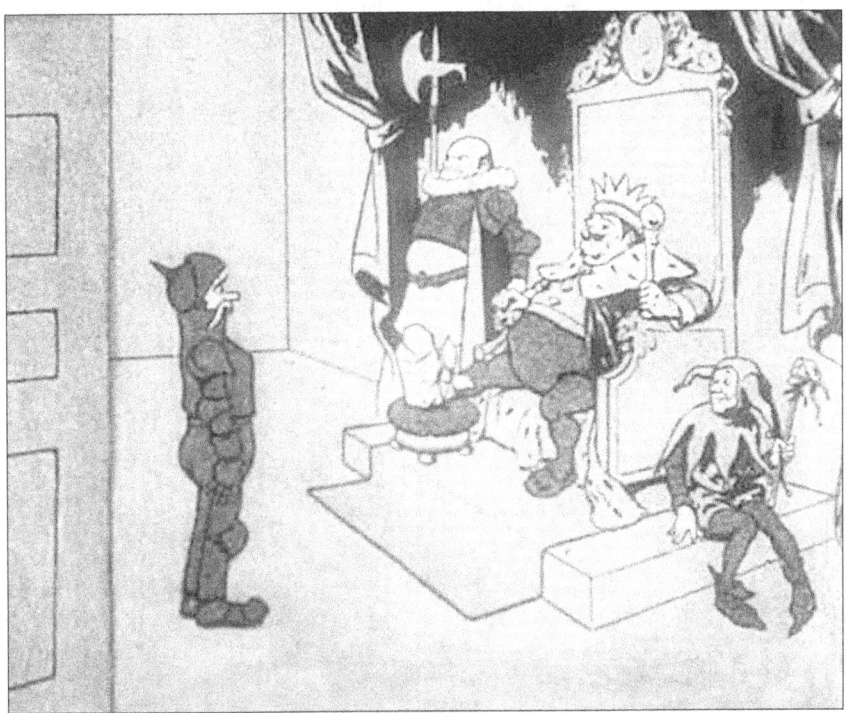

"Otto Luck" episode, 1917, by Wallace A. Carlson.

39

1920 Films

A-Hunting We Will Go, Flicker Flicker Little Star, Get to Work, Mixing Business with Pleasure, Ship Ahoy, The Broilers, There's a Reason, The Toreador. Up She Goes, Westward Ho, Accidents Will Happen, Andy's Inter-Ruben Guest, Andy's Picnic, Andy at Shady Rest, Andy Fights the High Cost of Living, Andy on Pleasure Bent, Andy on the Beach, Andy Redecorates His Flat, Andy the Actor, Andy the Chicken Farmer, Andy the Hero, Andy the Model, Equestrian Andy, Howdy Partner, Ice Box Episodes, Militant Min, Wim and Wigor, Dud, Lion Tamer, Andy and Min at the Theatre, Andy Visits the Osteopath, Andy's Night Out, Andy on a Diet, Andy's Mother-in-Law Pays Him a Visit, Andy's Wash Day, Andy on Skates, Andy Plays Golf, Andy Spends a Quiet Day at Home, Andy's Dancing Lesson, Andy Visits His Mamma-in-Law, Flat Hunting and Dud's Haircut.

1921 Films

Fatherly Love, The Chicken Thief, Andy's Dog Day, A Quiet Little Game, A Terrible Time, Jilted and Jolted, Andy's Cow, Andy's Holiday, Andy Has a Caller, Chester's Cat, Give 'Er the Gas, Rolling Around, The Best of Luck, The Masked Ball and The Promoters.

www.ingramcontent.com/pod-product-compliance
Lightning Source LLC
Chambersburg PA
CBHW071156220526
45468CB00003B/1056